Sonja Esbensen
Anna Rasmussen

Knitted Lace

Akacia

We would like to acknowledge the great help we have had from our loyal assistants

Ruth and Asta
Hanne J, Bodil and Hanne N

with knitting the designs

© Forlaget Akacia
Skovvænget 1
DK - 5690 Tommerup

Printed at InPrint, Riga, 2011

ISBN: 978-87-7847-046-1

Introduction

$\mathcal{W}$e met 12-13 years ago because we shared a hobby - knitted lace - and became friends. We had both been knitting for several years but we both lacked a friend to share our interest with. Purely by chance we heard about each other, got into touch and hit it off right away.

We are both interested in the old knitting patterns and our friendship marked the beginning of an interesting pursuit.
Through the years we have collected innumerable patterns from „Hjemmet" and „Nordisk Mønster Tidende". Nothing is as exciting as trying to decipher an old handwritten pattern: which materials do you have to use, how large is the finished work and how does it look? This turns into many enjoyable hours before the last stitch is cast off and the stretching can begin and you can enjoy the finished work in all its glory.

Knitted lace is a beautiful needlework, which also fits into a modern home.
With this book we want to open our treasure box with old patterns. This book contains 50 designs, large and small, easy and difficult between each other so there is something for everyone.

All of the designs are shown at photographs and the patterns are made with symbols. This should make it much easier to work with the book.

We hope you will enjoy the book,

Anna Rasmussen
Sonja Esbensen

Materials

All of the designs in this book are knitted with DMC Cébélia no. 10, 20 and 30.

Ordinary knitting needles have been used both double pointed needles and circular needles. It is better if the double pointed needles are short because it makes it easier to cast on the stitches. For the large designs up to one meter long, circular needles have been used.

The size of the designs can be altered if a thinner or a thicker yarn is used.. Remember to change the size of the knitting needles as well.

It is always a good idea to make a knitting sample before you start.

Reading a pattern

To make it as easy as possible to decipher a pattern they have all been made with symbols. The pattern

report is only shown one time. The report is repeated until the end of the round.
At the next pages you will find a description of all of the symbols and an explanation of how to read the patterns.

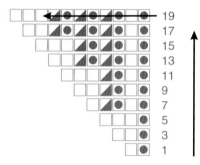

The patterns should be read as they are knitted, from the bottom to the top and from right to left.

In some patterns it has been necessary to describe a single round over more than one line. The same principle applies here: the pattern is read from the bottom to the top and from the right towards the left with just this exception - that the round continues on the line above (see the illustration below).

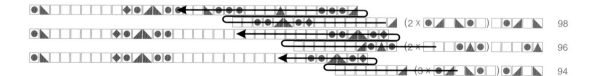

Remember: All rounds not mentioned in the pattern are **knitted plain.**

4

How to read the pattern

The following symbols are used for describing the patterns:

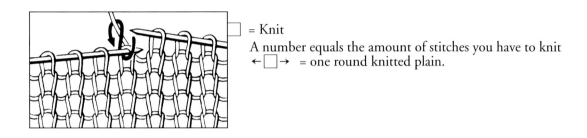

☐ = Knit

A number equals the amount of stitches you have to knit
←☐→ = one round knitted plain.

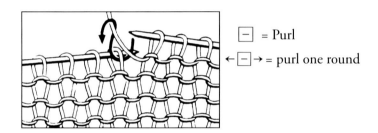

⊟ = Purl

←⊟→ = purl one round

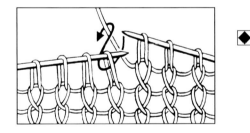

◆ = Knit 1 through back loop

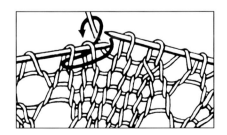

◢ = Knit 2 stitches together

▨3 ▨4 ▨5 ▨6 = Knit 3, 4, 5 or 6 stitches together

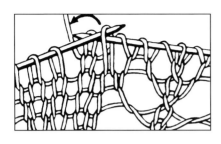

◣ = Slip 1 stitch, knit 1, pass slipped stitch over

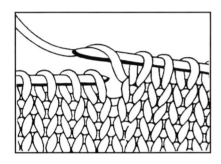

⬤ = Yarn over

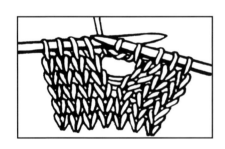

◕ = Yarn over 2, knit 1 and purl 1 into double yarn over on next row, if nothing else is mentioned at the design.

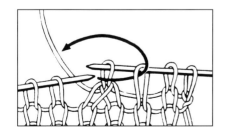

▲ = Slip 1 stitch, knit 2 together, pass slipped stitch over

⋂ = Slip 1 stitch, knit 3 together, pass slipped stitch over

▼ = Slip 2 stitches, knit 2, pass slipped stitch over

⊏ = Slip 3 stitches, knit 2, pass slipped stitches over

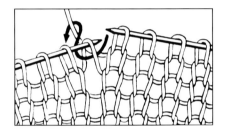

Ụ ② ③ ④ ⑤ = Knit 1, 2, 3, 4 or stitches back into running thread between 2 stitches from previuos round

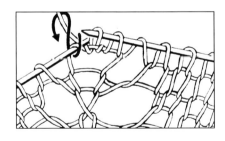

② ③ ④ ⑤ ⑥ ⑦ – Knit the number of stitches shown by numeral into the same stitch, alternating, knit, purl, etc.

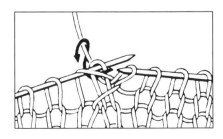

⊠ = Cross 2 stitches to the left: knit the 2nd stitch then knit the first stitch, and slip both stitches off the needle.

7

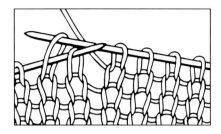 = Cross 2 stitches to the right: knit the 2nd stitch through back loop, then knit the first stitch, and slip both stitches off the needle

M = Stitch

X = Repeat. The numeral shows how many times the sequence has to be repeated.

← M = Slip one stitch from right to left. If there is also a numeral, (ex. ← 3M) slip that number of stitches

→ M = Slip one stitch from left to right. If there is also a numeral (ex. → 3M) slip that number of stitches

★ = "Note" See individual patterns for Notes

( ) = Repeat the pattern

How to start

1. The first stitch is formed by making a loop on the yarn and putting it onto the knitting needle.

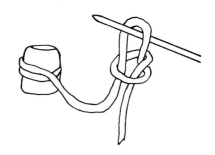

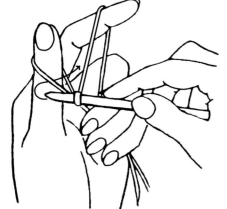

2. Pass the knitting needle under the yarn at the thumb.

3. Fetch the yarn at the forefinger with the needle. Now the second stitch is on the knitting needle.

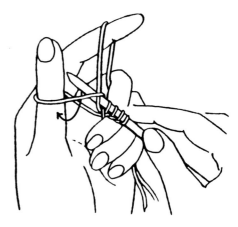

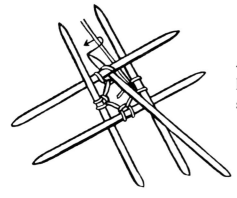

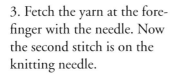

4. The illustration shows how to knit the first stitch in round 2.

5. At the beginning of the work it is a good idea to have a thread in another colour follow up through the work in order to mark the beginning of the round.

How to complete a work

Casting off

Loose cast off. If you knit too tightly it is an advantage to cast off with a knitting needle which is half a number larger than the ones used for the rest of the work. By doing this it can be avoided making the edge too tight.

Crocheting

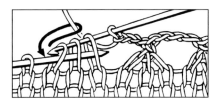

With models with a crochet edge the procedure is described with numbers. The numbers indicate the amount of stitches which are to be crocheted together and the amount of chain stitches between them.
The model at the illustration would be described like this:
3 stitches together with 4 chain stitches between.

Washing instructions

Wash the finished work thoroughly in order to get as much of the filling out of the yarn as posible so that it will accept the starch better.
I use a cornflower starch, which is made like this:
Mix 1 teaspoon starch with cold water. Add boiling water and mix the blend thoroughly. Take care that the blend does not get too thick. Let the mixture cool down until it is tepid. Then rinse the knitting with the starch and squeeze the starch through the knitting a couple of times in order to ensure that the starch is worked into the yarn. At last squeeze the knitting in a clean cloth and now it is ready for getting stretched. REMEMBER to use rustless pins.

Stretching

To ensure that the finished work presents itself as well as possible it has to be washed and pinned out. In most cases it is a great help, or rather a necessity, to make a paper pattern to ensure that the finished work attains the correct shape.
The paper pattern is made on a large piece of paper where the design is drawn in full size and where the finished work is stretched out while it is moist still.
Always draw with a pencil. Ink might rub off especially when the design is moist and it is difficult to remove again.

Place the moist design on the form and stretch it out with <u>stainless</u> pins. The stretching should be made as diagonally as possible - see the illustrations below.

Paper patterns

The paper patterns may be drawn on cardboard and used again.

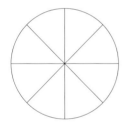

Circular forms.
Draw a circle in the correct size. You can also divide the circle into halves, quarters and eighths.

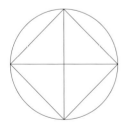

A four-sided form.
Divide the circle into quarters and draw a quadrangle.

A hexagonal form.
Draw the circles as illustrated below. The hexagonal emerges in the centre.

 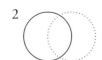 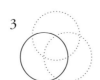 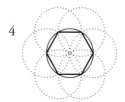 

Anna

Design "Anna"

Knitted with DMC Cébélia no. 20
Yarn requirement is about 20 gramme
The stretched size is about 40 centimetre
1 Set double pointed knitting needles 1.5 millimetre
1 Circular needle 1.5 millimetre at 40 and at 50 centimetre
1 Circular hook 1.25 millimetre

Crochet edge: Crochet 3 stitches together with 7 chain stitches between.

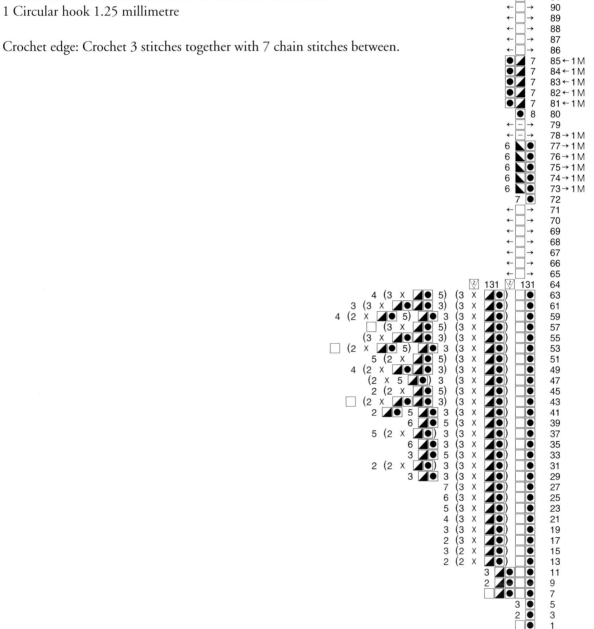

CAST ON 8 STITCHES AND KNIT ONE ROUND PLAIN.
ALL OF THE ROUNDS WHICH ARE NOT MENTIONED ARE KNITTED PLAIN.

Design "Anne Katrine"

Knitted with DMC Cébélia no. 20
Yarn requirement is about 15 gramme
The stretched size is about 30 centimetre
1 Set double pointed knitting needles 1.5 millimetre
1 Circular pin 1.5 millimetre at 40 centimetre
1 Crochet hook 1.25 millimetre

Crochet edge: 5-3 stitches knitted together with 7 chain stitches between.

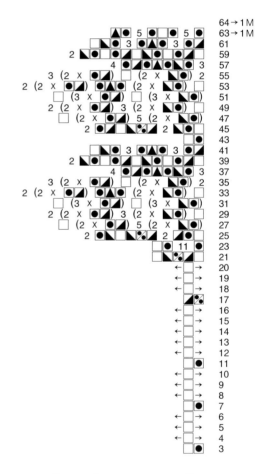

CAST ON 8 STITCHES AND KNIT 2 ROUNDS PLAIN.
ALL ROUNDS WHICH ARE NOT MENTIONED ARE KNITTED PLAIN.

Anne Katrine

Design "Annette"

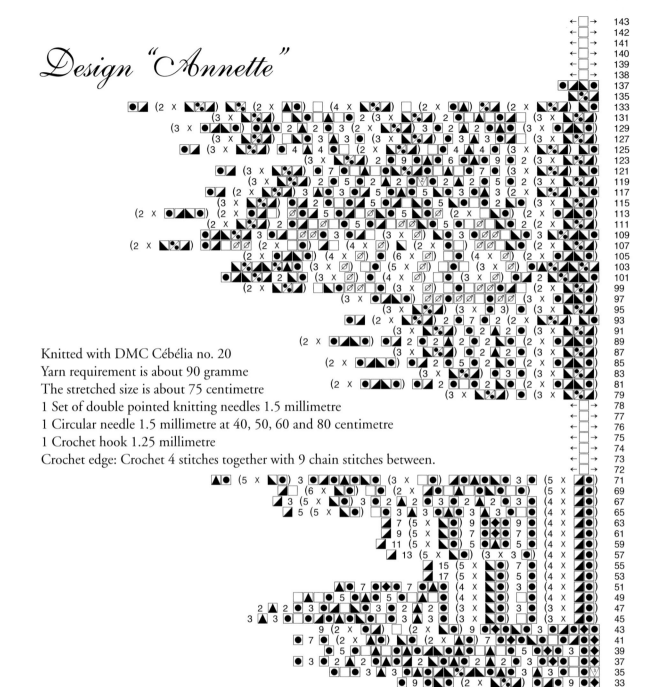

Knitted with DMC Cébélia no. 20

Yarn requirement is about 90 gramme

The stretched size is about 75 centimetre

1 Set of double pointed knitting needles 1.5 millimetre

1 Circular needle 1.5 millimetre at 40, 50, 60 and 80 centimetre

1 Crochet hook 1.25 millimetre

Crochet edge: Crochet 4 stitches together with 9 chain stitches between.

CAST ON 6 STITCHES AND KNIT 2 ROUNDS PLAIN.

ALL ROUNDS WHICH ARE NOT MENTIONED ARE KNITTED PLAIN.

Annette

Asta

Design "Asta"

Knitted with DMC Cébélia no. 30
Yarn requirement is about 15 gramme
The stretched size is about 28 centimetre
1 Set of double pointed knitting needles 1.5 millimetre
1 Circular needle 1.5 millimetre at 40 and 50 centimetre
1 Crochet hook 1.25 millimetre

Crochet edge:Crochet 3 stitches together with 7 chain stitches between.
Round 2: Crochet 8 chain stitches between the chains.

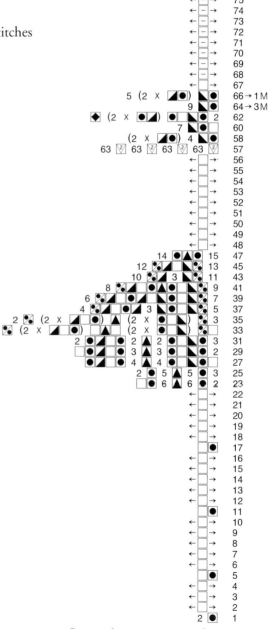

CAST ON 6 STITCHES AND KNIT 2 ROUNDS PLAIN.
ALL ROUNDS WHICH ARE NOT MENTIONED ARE KNITTED PLAIN.

19

Design "Bente"

Knitted with DMC Cébélia No. 20
Yarn requirement is about 25 gramme
The stretched size is about 32 x 46 centimetre
1 Set of double pointed knittings needles 1.5 millimetre
1 Circular needle 1.5 millimetre at 40, 50 and 60 centimetre
1 Crochet hook 1.25 millimetre

PATTERN **A**

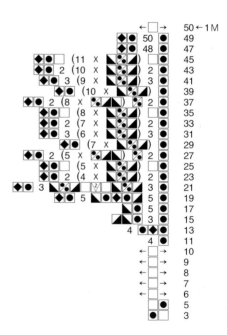

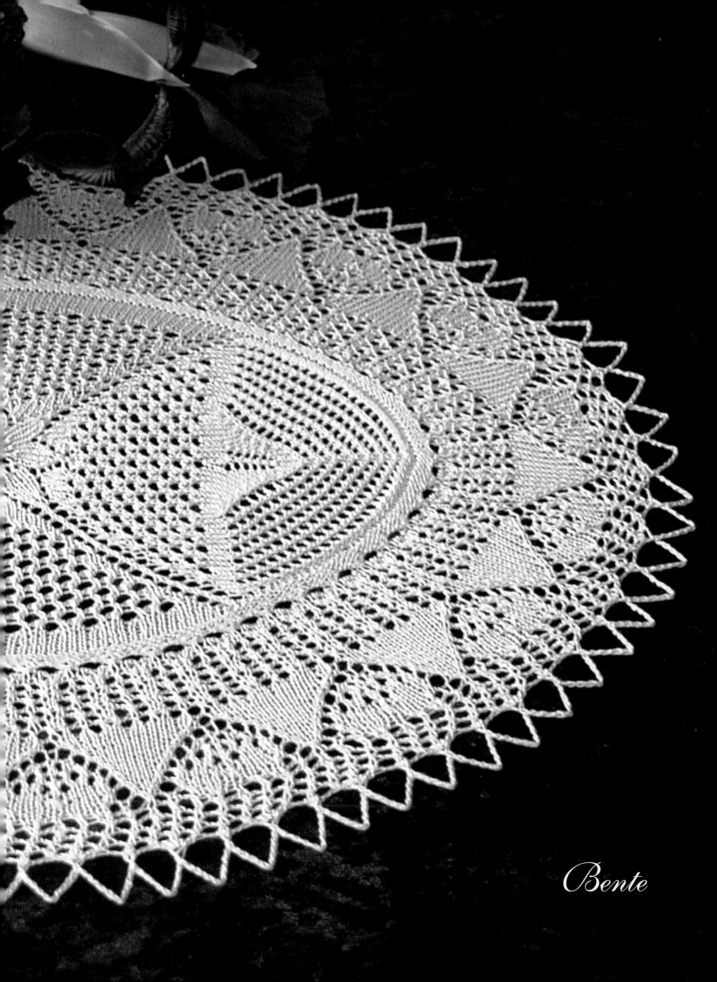

Bente

PATTERN B

Take up the stitches like this: 4 stitches from the top of the point, 32 stitches from one of the long sides of the point, 52 stitches from the stitchholder, 32 stitches from the long side of the other point, 4 stitches from the top of the point, 32 stitches from the other long side of the point, 52 stitches from the second stitchholder and finally 32 stitches from the long side of the point. A total of 240 stitches. After this one round is knitted plain before starting pattern C.

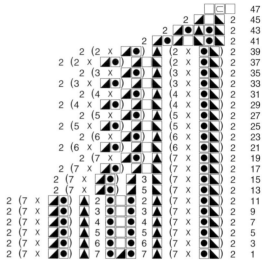

Then the stitches are distributed as follows: 54 stitches to the first point **pattern B,** 52 stitches on a stitchholder, first long side 54 stitches to the second point, **pattern B** and 52 stitches on a stitchholder for the second long side of the point.

PATTERN C - THE EDGE

Crochet edge: Crochet 3-5-3-5 stitches with 9 chain stitches between.

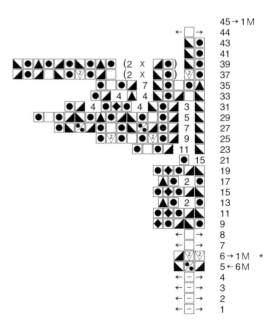

* = In round 6 - pattern C - ☑☑ knit down
   into yarn over 2 in round 5

Design "Birthe"

Knitted with DMC Cébélia No. 20
Yarn requirement is about 35 gramme
The stretched out size is about 50 centimetre
1 Set of double pointed knitting needles 1.5 millimetre
1 Circular needle 1.5 millimetre at 40, 50 and 60 centimetre
1 Crochet hook 1.25 millimetre

Crochet edge: Crochet 2-2-5-2 stitches with 7 chain stitches
between, 2 stitches together + 1 chain stitch, 3 stitches together +
1 chain stitch.

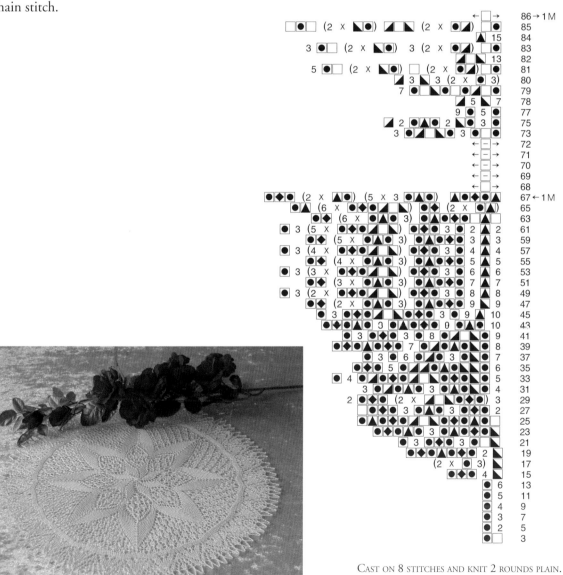

CAST ON 8 STITCHES AND KNIT 2 ROUNDS PLAIN.
ALL ROUNDS WHICH ARE NOT MENTIONED ARE
KNITTED PLAIN.

Design "Cecilie"

Knitted with DMC Cébélia No. 30
Yarn requirement is about 10 gramme
The stretched out size is about 18 centimetre
1 Set of double pointed knitting needles 1.5 millimetre
1 Crochet hook 1.25 millimetre

Crochet edge: Crochet 4-4-3-4-4 stitches together with 7 chain stitches between + 1 double crochet, crochet 3 stitches together + 1 double crochet.

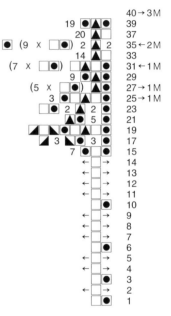

CAST ON 6 STITCHES AND KNIT ONE
ROUND PLAIN.
ALL ROUNDS WHICH ARE NOT MEN-
TIONED ARE KNITTED PLAIN.

Design "Charlotte"

Knitted with DMC Cébélia No. 10
Yarn requirement is about 25 gramme
The stretched size is about 24 x 24 centimetre
1 Set of fine knitting needles 1.5 millimetre
1 Circular needle 1.5 millimetre at 40 and 50 centimetre
1 Crochet hook 1.25 millimetre

Crochet edge: Crochet 1 stitch off with 1 chain stitch
between, then crochet 1 round of
picots like this: crochet 3 chain
stitches + 1 double chrochet in
the first chain stitch and then one
slipstitch in the second stitch.

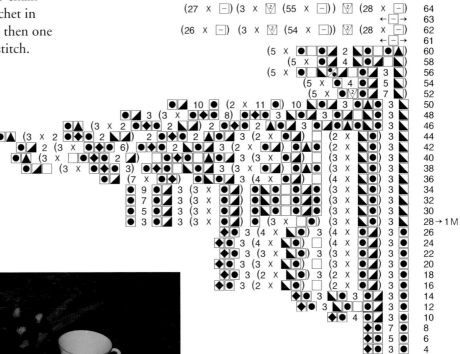

CAST ON 8 STITCHES AND KNIT 1 ROUND PLAIN.
ALL ROUNDS WHICH ARE NOT MENTIONED ARE
KNITTED PLAIN.

Design "Ditte I"

Knitted with DMC Cébélia No. 20
Yarn requirement is about 6 gramme
The stretched size is about 17 centimetre
1 Set of double pointed knitting needles 1.5 millimetre
1 Crochet hook 1.25 millimetre

Crochet edge: Crochet 2-3 stitches together with 7 chain stitches between.

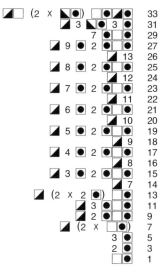

CAST ON 8 STITCHES AND KNIT
1 ROUND PLAIN.
ALL ROUNDS WHICH ARE NOT
MENTIONED ARE KNITTED PLAIN.

26

Design "Ditte II"

Knitted with DMC Cébélia No. 20
Yarn requirement is about 30 gramme
The stretched size is about 40 centimetre
1 Set of double pointed knitting needles 1.5 millimetre
1 Circular needle 1.5 millimetre at 40, 50 and 60 centimetre
1 Crochet hook 1.25 millimetre
Crochet edge: Crochet 3 stitches together with 7 chain stitches between.

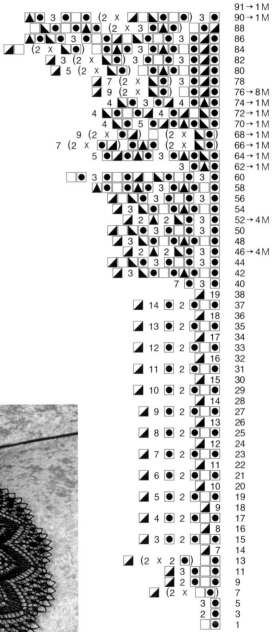

CAST ON 8 STITCHES AND KNIT
ONE ROUND PLAIN.
ALL ROUNDS WHICH ARE NOT
MENTIONED ARE KNITTED PLAIN.

Design "Elly"

Knitted with DMC Cébélia No. 20
Yarn requirement is about 7 gramme
The stretched size is about 20 centimetre
1 Set of double pointed knitting needles 1.5 millimetre
Crochet hook 1.25 millimetre

Crochet edge: Crochet 3 stitches together with 7 chain stitches between.

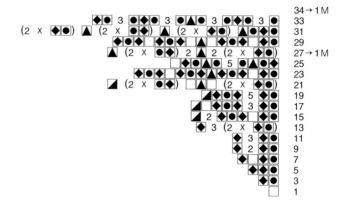

CAST ON 7 STITCHES AND KNIT
ONE ROUND PLAIN.
ALL ROUNDS WHICH ARE NOT
MENTIONED ARE KNITTED PLAIN.

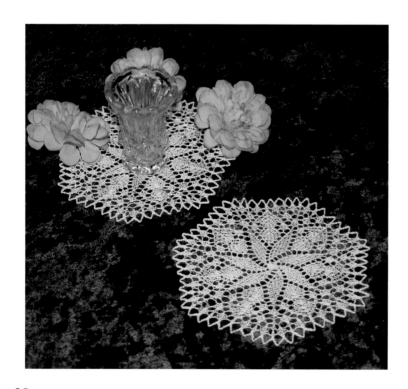

28

Design "Gerda"

Knitted with DMC Cébélia No. 30
Yarn requirement is about 6 gramme
The stretched size is about 20 centimetre
1 Set of double pointed knitting needles 1.5 millimetre
1 Circular needle 1.5 millimetre at 40 centimetre
1 Crochet hook 1.25 millimetre

Crochet edge: Crochet 4 stitches together with 9 chain stitches between.

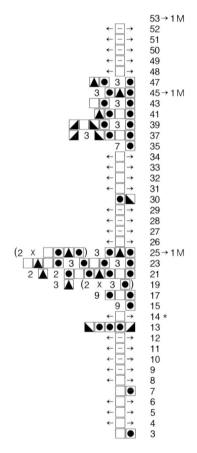

CAST ON 8 STITCHES AND KNIT 2 ROUNDS PLAIN.
ALL ROUNDS WHICH ARE NOT MENTIONED ARE
KNITTED PLAIN.

*= In round 14 7 stitches are knitted from the 3 yarn over.

Design "Gitte I"

Knitted with DMC Cébélia No. 20
Yarn requirement is about 5 gramme
The stretched size is about 15 centimetre
1 Set of double pointed knitting needles 1.5 millimetre
1 Crochet hook 1.25 millimetre

Crochet edge: Crochet 3 stitches together with 7 chain
stitches between.

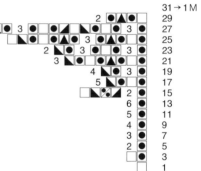

CAST ON 8 STITCHES AND KNIT
ONE ROUND PLAIN.
ALL ROUNDS WHICH ARE NOT
MENTIONED ARE KNITTED PLAIN.

Design "Gitte II"

Knitted with DMC Cébélia No. 20
Yarn requirement is about 30 gramme
The stretched size is about 45 centimetre
1 Set of double pointed knitting needles 1.5 millimetre
1 Circular needle 1.5 millimetre at 40, 50 and 60 centimetre
1 Crochet hook 1.25 millimetre

Crochet edge: Crochet 4-3 stitches together with 7 chain stitches between.

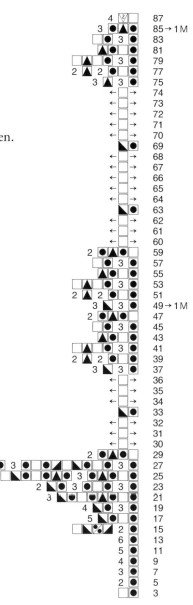

CAST ON 8 STITCHES AND KNIT
2 ROUNDS PLAIN.
ALL ROUNDS WHICH ARE NOT
MENTIONED ARE KNITTED PLAIN

31

Design "Grethe"

Knitted with DMC Cébélia No. 30
Yarn requirement is about 30 gramme
The stretched size is about 45 centimetre
1 Set of double pointed knitting needles 1.5 millimetre
1 Circular needle 1.5 millimetre at 40, 50 and 60 centimetre
1 Crochet hook 1.25 millimetre

Crochet edge: Crochet 4 stitches together with 7 chain
stitches between.

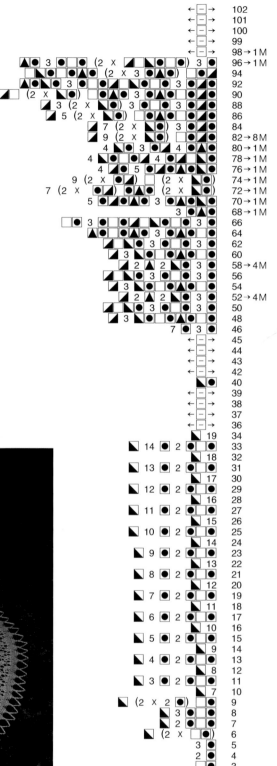

CAST ON 8 STITCHES AND KNIT 2 ROUNDS PLAIN.
ALL ROUNDS WHICH ARE NOT MENTIONED ARE
KNITTED PLAIN.

Design "Heidi"

Knitted with DMC Cébélia No. 30
Yarn requirement is about 6 gramme
The stretched size is about 39 centimetre
1 Set of fine knitting needles 1.5 millimetre
1 Crochet hook 1.25 millimetre

Crochet edge: Crochet 3 stitches together with
7 chain stitches between.

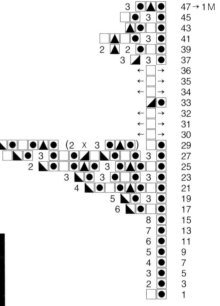

CAST ON 8 STITCHES AND KNIT 1
ROUND PLAIN.
ALL ROUNDS WHICH ARE NOT
MENTIONED ARE KNITTED PLAIN.

Design "Ingeborg I"

Knitted with DMC Cébélia No. 20
Yarn requirement is about 5 gramme
The stretched size is about 14 centimetre
1 Set of double pointed knitting needles 1.5 millimetre
1 Crochet hook 1.25 millimetre

Crochet edge: Crochet 5-4-4-5-4-4-5 stitches together with 9 chain stitches between, 3 stitches with 3 chain stitches between twice, 3 stitches with 9 chain stitches between.

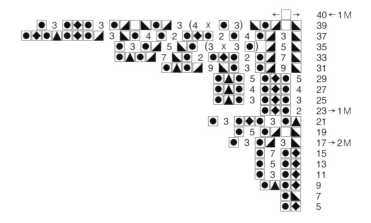

CAST ON 8 STICHES AND KNIT
4 ROUNDS PLAIN.
ALL ROUNDS WHICH ARE NOT
MENTIONED ARE KNITTED
PLAIN.

Design "Ingeborg II"

Knitted with DMC Cébélia No. 20
Yarn requirement is about 12 gramme
The stretched size is about 22 centimetre
1 Set of double pointed knitting needles 1.5 millimetre
1 Circular needle 1.5 millimetre at 40 centimetre
1 Crochet hook 1.25 millimetre

Crochet edge: Crochet 5-5-5-4-5-4-5-5-5-3-3 stitches together with 9 chain stitches between.
3 stitches with 1 chain stitch between twice, 3 stitches with 9 chain stitches between 3 times.

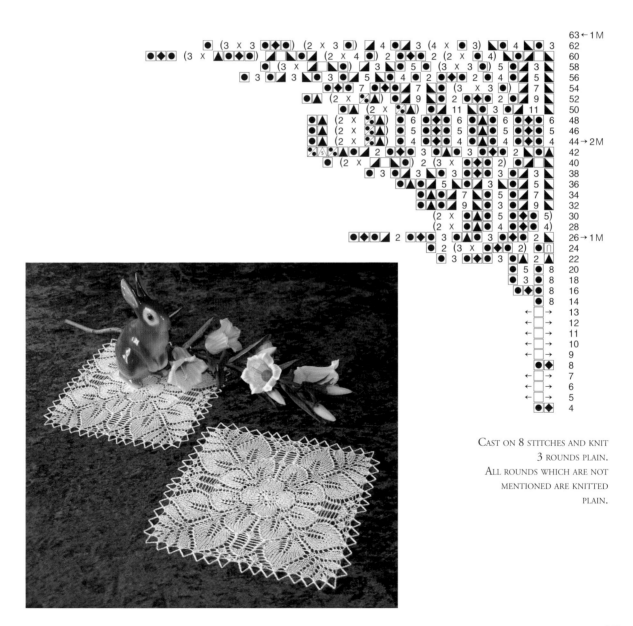

Cast on 8 stitches and knit
3 rounds plain.
All rounds which are not
mentioned are knitted
plain.

35

Jette

Design "Jette"

Knitted with DMC Cébélia No. 20
Yarn requirement is about 20 gramme
The stretched size is about 39 centimetre
1 Set of double pointed knitting needles 1.5 millimetre
1 Circular needle 1.5 millimetre at 40 centimetre
1 Crochet hook 1.25 millimetre

Crochet edge: Crochet 3 stitches together with 7 chain stitches between.

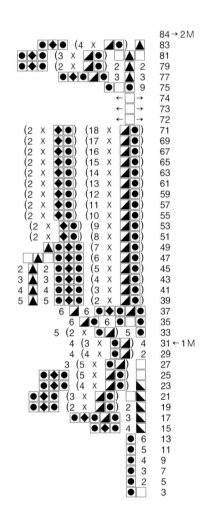

CAST ON 6 OR 8 STITCHES, DEPENDING ON HOW LARGE A DOILY
YOU WANT, AND KNIT 2 ROUNDS PLAIN.
ALL ROUNDS WHICH ARE NOT MENTIONED ARE KNITTED PLAIN.

Design "Jonna"

Knitted with DMC Cébélia No. 30
Yarn requirement is about 12 gramme
The stretched size is about 22x30 centimetre
1 Set of double pointed knitting needles 1.5 millimetre
1 Circular needle 1.5 millimetre
1 Crochet hook 1.25 millimetre

PATTERN A

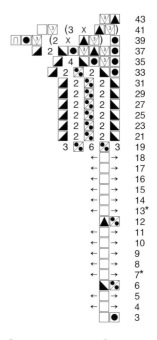

Cast on 9 stitches and knit 2 rounds plain.
All rounds which are not mentioned are knitted plain.

* = In round 7 and round 13 5 stitches are knitted into
   double yarn over.

PATTERN B

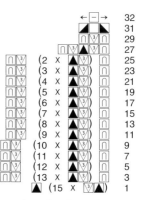

Here the stitches are distributed like this: 2 x 63 stitches for points and 2 x 81 stitches for the sides.
Purl back.

Pattern **C** - the edge

All stitches are cast off with a needle which is 0.5 millimetre larger than the one the work is knitted with in order not to make the edge too tight.

*In round 8 in pattern C 3 stitches are knit-
   ted into yarn over 2 in round 7

The stitches are now picked up around the doily like this: 40 stitches along the first point, 81 stitches from the side, 40 stitches along the other point, 3 stitches at the top, 40 stitches along the other side, 81 stitches from the other side, 40 stitches along the last point, 3 stitches at the top. A total of 328 stitches.

Jutta

Design "Jutta"

Knitted with DMC Cébélia No. 20
Yarn requirement is about 22 gramme
The stretched size is about 40 centimetre
1 Set of double pointed knitting needles 1.5 millimetre
1 Circular needle 1.5 millimetre at 40 and 50 centimetre
1 Crochet hook 1.25 millimetre

Crochet edge: crochet 4-3-3-3 stitches together with 7 chain
stitches between, 4 stitches together + 1 chain stitch, 6 stitches
together + 1 chain stitch.

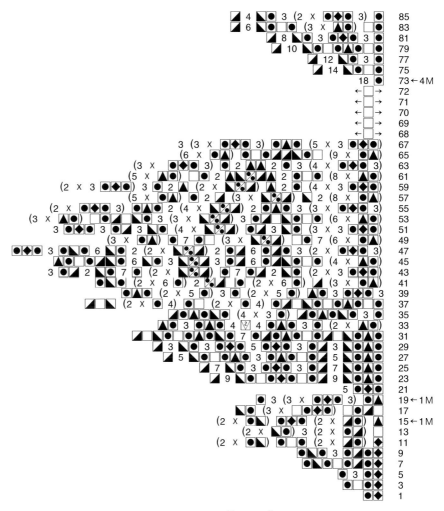

CAST ON 6 STITCHES AND KNIT ONE ROUND PLAIN.
ALL ROUNDS WHICH ARE NOT MENTIONED ARE KNITTED PLAIN.

Karen

Design "Karen"

Knitted with DMC Cébélia No. 30
Yarn requirement is about 50 gramme
The stretched size is about 57 centimetre
1 Set of double pointed knitting needles 1.5 millimetre
1 Circular needle at 40, 60 and 80 centimetre
1 Crochet hook 1.25 millimetre

to be continued...

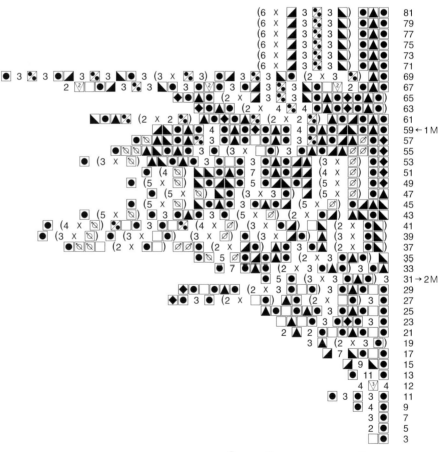

CAST ON 8 STITCHES AND KNIT 2 ROUNDS PLAIN.
ALL ROUNDS WHICH ARE NOT MENTIONED ARE
KNITTED PLAIN.

Crochet edge: Crochet 5 stitches together + 1 chain stitch, 3 stitches with 7 chain stitches between 5 times, 3 stitches + 1 chain stitch, 5 stitches + 1 chain stitch.

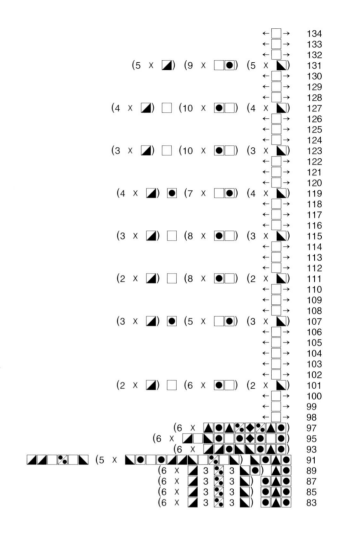

← □ →	134
← □ →	133
← □ →	132
(5 x ◣) (9 x □●) (5 x ◢)	131
← □ →	130
← □ →	129
← □ →	128
(4 x ◣) □ (10 x ●□) (4 x ◢)	127
← □ →	126
← □ →	125
← □ →	124
(3 x ◣) □ (10 x ●□) (3 x ◢)	123
← □ →	122
← □ →	121
← □ →	120
(4 x ◣) ● (7 x □●) (4 x ◢)	119
← □ →	118
← □ →	117
← □ →	116
(3 x ◣) □ (8 x ●□) (3 x ◢)	115
← □ →	114
← □ →	113
← □ →	112
(2 x ◣) □ (8 x ●□) (2 x ◢)	111
← □ →	110
← □ →	109
← □ →	108
(3 x ◣) ● (5 x □●) (3 x ◢)	107
← □ →	106
← □ →	105
← □ →	104
← □ →	103
← □ →	102
(2 x ◣) □ (6 x ●□) (2 x ◢)	101
← □ →	100
← □ →	99
← □ →	98
(6 x ◣●◢●◣◆●◆◢●◢●)	97
(6 x ◣◢ ●◢◆◢◣◣●◢●)	95
(6 x ◢◢◣◣◢●◣●)	93
◢◢ ⠿ ◣ (5 x ◣●□ ●◣◢ ⠿ ◣) ●◣◢●	91
(6 x ◢ 3 ⠿ 3 ◣) ●◣◢●	89
(6 x ◢ 3 ⠿ 3 ◣) ●◢◣●	87
(6 x ◢ 3 ⠿ 3 ◣) ●◢◣●	85
(6 x ◢ 3 ⠿ 3 ◣) ●◣◢●	83

...continued

Design "Kaya"

Knitted with DMC Cébélia No. 20
Yarn requirement is about 7 gramme
The stretched size is about 18 centimetre
1 Set of double pointed knitting needles 1.5 millimetre
1 Crochet hook 1.25 millimetre

Crochet edge: Crochet 3 stitches together with 6 chain stitches between.
Round 2: Start at the middle of the first chain and crochet 7 chain stitches between each chain.
Round 3: Start at the middle of the first chain and crochet 7 chain stitches between each chain.

Kirsten

Design "Kirsten"

Knitted with DMC Cébélia No. 20
Yarn requirement is about 35 gramme
The stretched size is about 47 centimetre
1 Set fine knitting needles 1.5 millimetre
1 Circular needle 1.5 millimetre at 40 and 60 centimetre
1 Crochet hook 1.25 millimetre

Crochet edge: Crochet 4-3-3-3-3-3-3-3 stitches together with 7
chain stitches between, 3 stitches + 1 chain stitch.

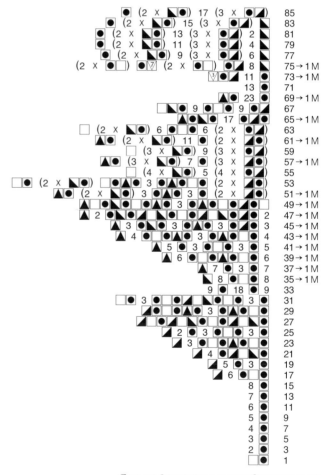

Cast on 9 stitches and knit 2 rounds plain.
All rounds which are not mentioned are knitted plain.

Design "Lerke I"

Knitted with DMC Cébélia No. 20
Yarn requirement is about 5 gramme
The stretched size is about 18 centimetre
1 Set of double pointed knitting needles 1.5 millimetre
1 Crochet hook 1.25 millimetre

Crochet edge: Crochet 4-3-3-3-3-4-3 stitches together with
7 chain stitches between.

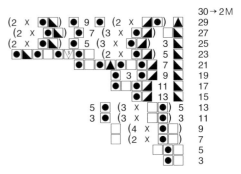

CAST ON 6 STITCHES AND KNIT 2 ROUNDS PLAIN.
ALL ROUNDS WHICH ARE NOT MENTIONED ARE
KNITTED PLAIN.

Design "Lerke II"

Knitted with DMC Cébélia No. 20
Yarn requirement is about 10 gramme
The stretched size is about 23 centimetre
1 Set of double pointed knitting needles 1.5 millimetre
1 Crochet hook 1.25 millimetre

Crochet edge: Crochet 4-3-3-5-3-3-4-3 stitches together with
9 chain stitches between.

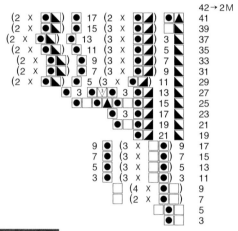

CAST ON 6 STITCHES AND KNIT
2 ROUNDS PLAIN.
ALL ROUNDS WHICH ARE NOT
MENTIONED ARE KNITTED
PLAIN.

Design "Lerke III"

Knitted with DMC Cébélia No. 20
Yarn requirement is about 15 gramme
The stretched size is about 32 centimetre
1 Set of double pointed knitting needles 1.5 millimtre
1 Circular needle 1.5 millimetre at 40 centimetre
1 Crochet hook 1.25 millimetre

Crochet edge: Crochet 4-3-3-3-3-3-4-3 stitches together
with 9 chain stitches between.

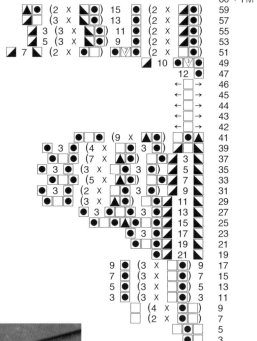

CAST ON 6 STITCHES AND KNIT 2
ROUNDS PLAIN.
ALL ROUNDS WHICH ARE NOT
MENTIONED ARE KNITTED PLAIN.

Design "Lis"

Knitted with DMC Cébélia No. 20
Yarn requirement is about 10 gramme
The stretched size is about 24 centimetre
1 Set of double pointed knitting needles 1.5 millimetre
1 Crochet hook 1.25 millimetre

Crochet edge: Crochet 4-2-3-2-4-3 stitches together with
7 chain stitches between.

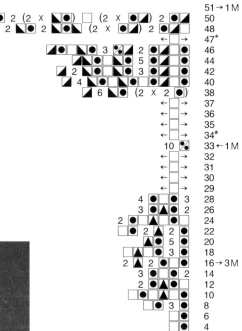

CAST ON 10 STITCHES AND KNIT 3
ROUNDS PLAIN.
ALL ROUNDS WHICH ARE NOT MEN-
TIONED ARE KNITTED PLAIN.

*** = In round 34 and 47 knit 4
stitches in the double yarn over.**

Design „Lisbeth"

Knitted with DMC Cébélia No. 20
Yarn requirement is about 65 gramme
The stretched size is about 70 centimetre
1 Set of double pointed knitting needles 1.5 millimetre
1 Circular needle 1.5 millimetre at 40, 50, 60 and 80 centimetre
1 Crochet hook 1.25 millimetre

Crochet edge: Crochet 4-3-3-3-5-3-4-6-6-5-6-5-6-3 -5-3-3-3-4-7 stitches together with 7 chain stitches between.

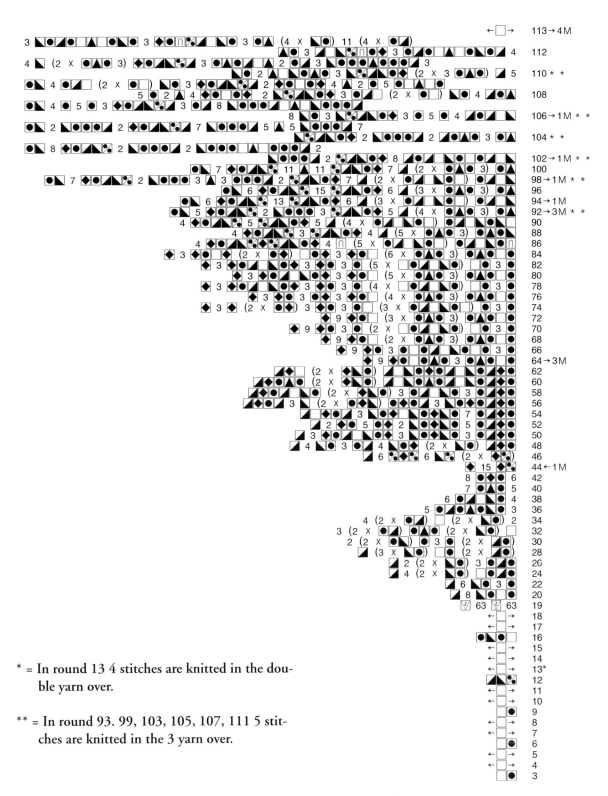

* = In round 13 4 stitches are knitted in the double yarn over.

** = In round 93. 99, 103, 105, 107, 111 5 stitches are knitted in the 3 yarn over.

CAST ON 8 STITCHES AND KNIT 2 ROUNDS PLAIN.
ALL ROUNDS WHICH ARE NOT MENTIONED ARE KNITTED PLAIN

Lise-Lotte

Design "Lise-Lotte"

to be continued...

Knitted with DMC Cébélia No. 30
Yarn requirement is about 70 gramme
The stretched size is about 60 centimetre
1 Set of double pointed knitting needles 1.5 millimetre
1 Circular needle 1.5 millimetre at 40, 60, 80 and 100 centimetre
1 Crochet hook 1.25 millimetre

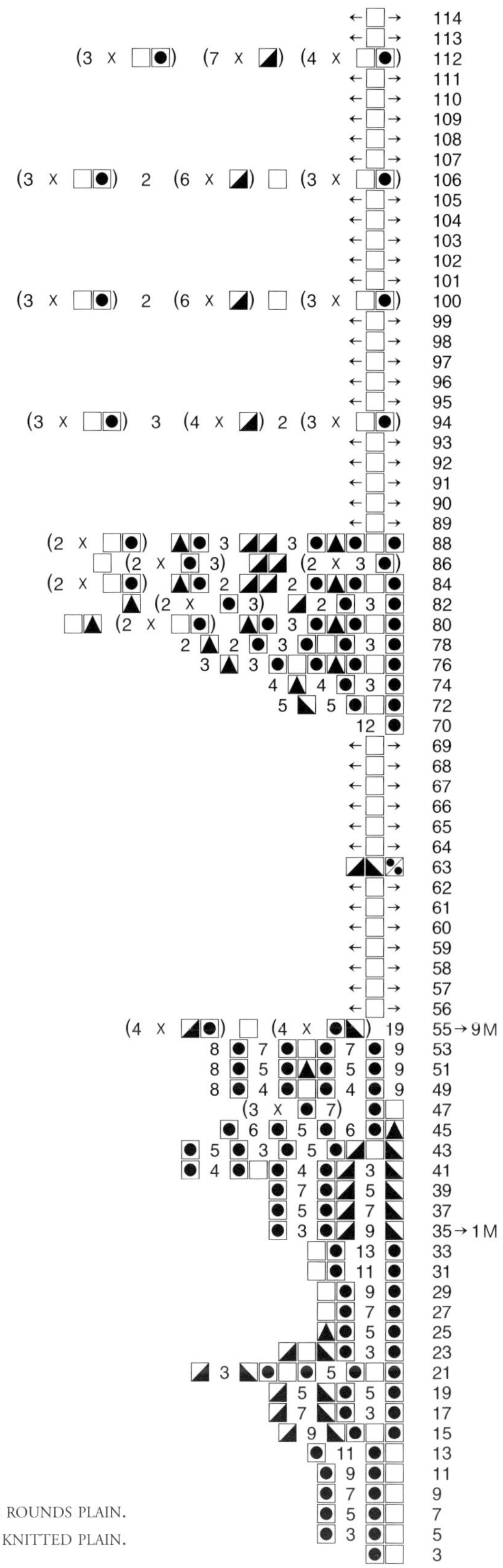

Cast on 8 stitches and knit 2 rounds plain.
All rounds which are not mentioned are knitted plain.

Crochet edge: Crochet 3-3-3-3 stitches together with 7 chain stitches between, 3 stitches
+ 1 chain stitch, 4 stitches + 1 chain stitch, 3
stitches + 1 chain stitch, crochet 3-3-3-3 stitches together with 7 chain stitches between.

← □ →	195
← □ →	194
← □ →	193
← □ →	192
← □ →	191
(6 x □●) (11 x ◢) ● (5 x □●)	190
← □ →	189
← □ →	188
← □ →	187
← □ →	186
← □ →	185
(5 x □●) □ (10 x ◢) (6 x □●)	184
← □ →	183
← □ →	182
← □ →	181
← □ →	180
← □ →	179
(5 x □●) (10 x ◢) (6 x □●)	178
← □ →	177
← □ →	176
← □ →	175
← □ →	174
← □ →	173
(5 x □●) (10 x ◢) ● (5 x □●)	172
← □ →	171
← □ →	170
← □ →	169
← □ →	168
← □ →	167
(5 x □●) □ (9 x ◢) (5 x □●)	166
← □ →	165
← □ →	164
← □ →	163
← □ →	162
← □ →	161
(5 x □●) (9 x ◢) (5 x □●)	160
← □ →	159
← □ →	158
← □ →	157
← □ →	156
← □ →	155
(5 x □●) (9 x ◢) ● (4 x □●)	154
← □ →	153
← □ →	152
← □ →	151
← □ →	150
← □ →	149
(4 x □●) □ (8 x ◢) (5 x □●)	148
← □ →	147
← □ →	146
← □ →	145
← □ →	144
← □ →	143
(4 x □●) (8 x ◢) (5 x □●)	142
← □ →	141
← □ →	140
← □ →	139
← □ →	138
← □ →	137
(4 x □●) (8 x ◢) ● (4 x □●)	136
← □ →	135
← □ →	134
← □ →	133
← □ →	132
← □ →	131
(4 x □●) (8 x ◢) (4 x □●)	130
← □ →	129
← □ →	128
← □ →	127
← □ →	126
← □ →	125
(4 x □●) □ (6 x ◢) 2 ● (3 x □●)	124
← □ →	123
← □ →	122
← □ →	121
← □ →	120
← □ →	119
← □ →	117
← □ →	115

...continued

56

Design "Majbritt I"

Knitted with DMC Cébélia No. 20
Yarn requirement is about 12 gramme
The stretched size is about 23 centimetre
1 Set of double pointed knitting needles 1.5 millimetre
1 Circular needle 1.5 millimetre at 40 centimetre
1 Crochet hook 1.25 millimetre

Crochet edge: Crochet 3 stitches together with 7 chain stithes between.

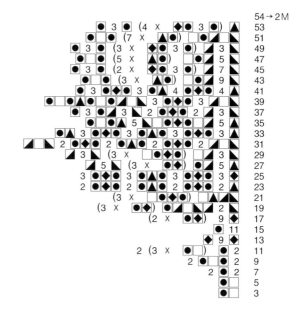

CAST ON 8 STITCHES AND KNIT 1 ROUND PLAIN. ALL ROUNDS WHICH ARE NOT MENTIONED ARE KNITTED PLAIN.

Design "Majbritt II"

Knitted with DMC Cébélia No. 20
Yarn requirement is about 115 gramme
The stretched size is about 79 centimetre
1 Set of fine knitting needles 1.5 millimetre
1 Circular needle 1.5 millimetre at 40, 50, 60, 80 and 100 centimetre
1 Crochet hook 1.25 millimetre

to be continued...

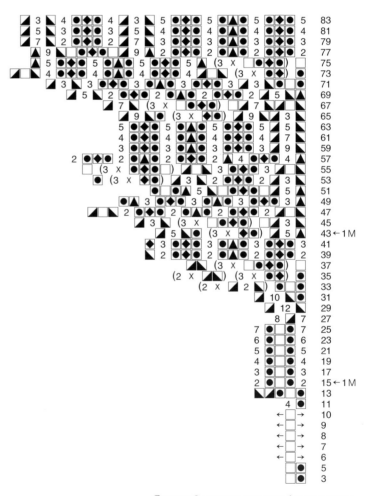

CAST ON 8 STITCHES AND KNIT 1 ROUND PLAIN.
ALL ROUNDS WHICH ARE NOT MENTIONED ARE KNITTED PLAIN.

Majbritt II

Crochet edge: Crochet 4 stitches together with 9 chain stitches between.

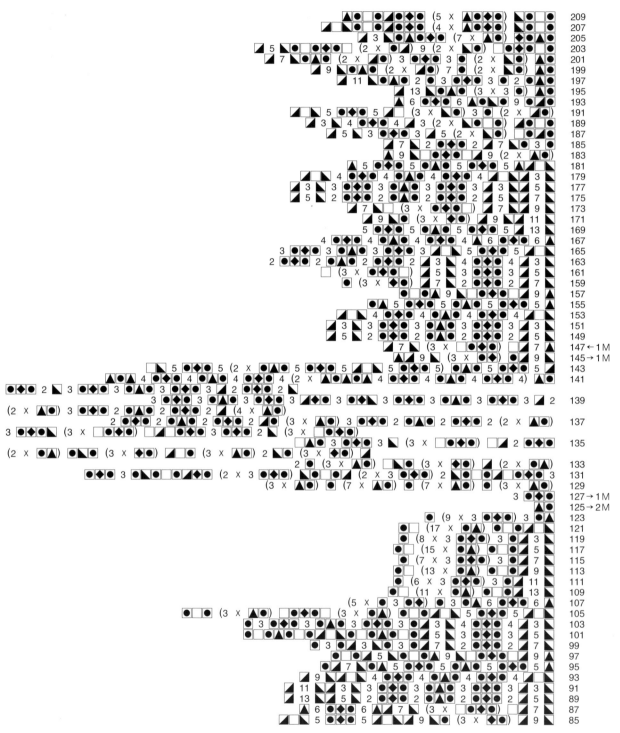

...continued

Design "Majken"

Knitted with DMC Cébélia No. 20
Yarn requirement is about 21 gramme
The stretched size is about 30 centimetre
1 Set of double pointed knitting needles 1.5 millimetre
1 Circular needle 1.5 millimetre at 40 and 50 centimetre
1 Crochet hook 1.25 millimetre

Crochet edge: Crochet 5-3-3-3 stitches together with 7 chain stitches together.

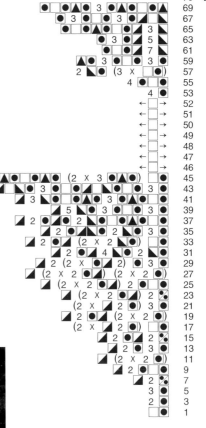

Cast on 8 stitches and knit
one round plain.
All rounds which are not
mentioned are knitted plain.

Design "Marie"

Knitted with DMC Cébélia No. 20
Yarn requirement is about 15 gramme
The stretched size is about 31 centimetre
1 Set of double pointed knitting needles 1.5 millimetre
1 Circular needle 1.5 millimetre at 40 centimetre
1 Crochet hook 1.25 millimetre

Crochet edge: Crochet 3 stitches together with 7 chain stitches between.

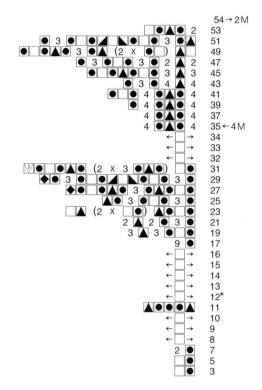

CAST ON 8 STITCHES AND KNIT 2 ROUNDS PLAIN.
ALL ROUNDS WHICH ARE NOT MENTIONED ARE KNITTED PLAIN.

* = In round 12 knit 7 stitches in the 3 yarn over.

Marie

Design "Mia"

Knitted with DMC Cébélia No. 20
Yarn requirement is about 70 gramme
The stretched size is about 75 centimetre
1 Set of double pointed knitting needles 1.5 millimetre
1 Circular needle 1.5 millimetre at 40, 50, 60 and 80 centimetre
1 Crochet hook 1.25 millimetre

Crochet edge: Crochet 3-3-3-4-4-4 stitches together with 7 chain stitches between.

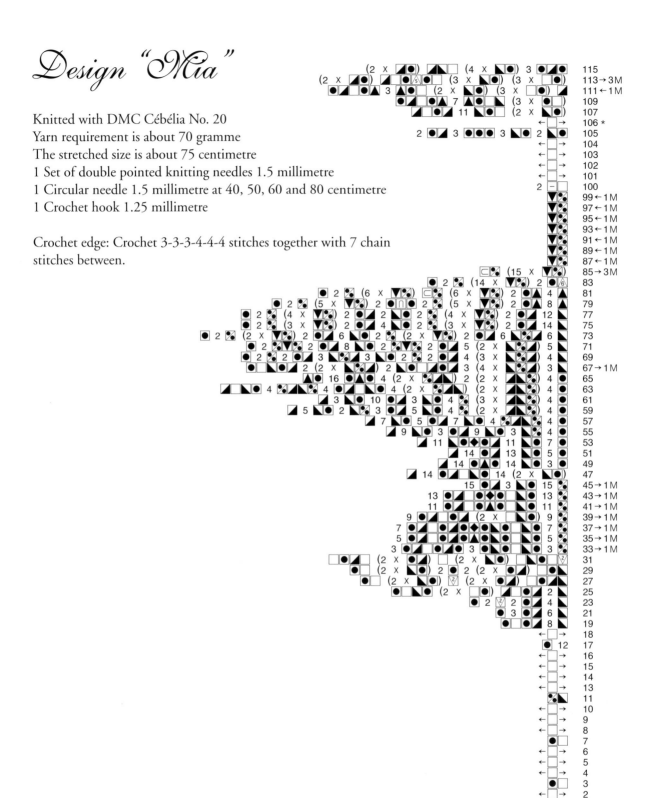

* = In round 106 knit 7 stitches in the 3 yarn over.

CAST ON 8 STITCHES AND KNIT ONE ROUND PLAIN.
ALL ROUNDS WHICH ARE NOT MENTIONED ARE KNITTED PLAIN

Design "Mona"

Knitted with DMC Cébélia No. 30
Yarn requirement is about 6 gramme
The stretched size is about 18 centimetre
1 Set of double pointed knitting needles 1.5 millimetre
1 Circular needle 1.5 millimetre at 40 centimetre
1 Crochet hook 1.25 millimetre

Crochet edge: Crochet 3-3-3-5-3-3-3-3 stitches together with 7
chain stitches between.

□ ● ▲ ● 3 ● ▲ ● (2 x □ ● ▲ ●) 3 ● ▲ ● ▲	45
● 3 ● ● 3 ● ◣ □ ● 3 ● □ ● 3 ● ▲ 2	43
● ● ▲ ● ◣ 3 ● 3 ● ● ▲ ● ▲ 4	41
● 3 ● ◣ 5 ● ◣ ● 3 ● 5	39
● ● ◣ 2 ◣ (2 x ● ◣) (2 x □ ●) 7	37
● 3 (3 x ● ◣) 2 ● (2 x ● ◣) ◣	35
● 3 (2 x ● ◣) 2 ● (3 x ● ◣) 2	33
● 7 ● 2 (3 x ● ◣) □	31
● 5 ● ◣ 2 (2 x ● ◣) 2	29
● 3 ● 8 ◣	27
● ● 9 ◣	25
● 12	23
● 11	21
● 4 (2 x ● ◣) 2	19
● 2 (3 x ● ◣) □	17
● 2 (2 x ● ◣) 2	15
● 7	13
● 6	11
● 5	9
● 4	7
● 3	5
● 2	3
● □	1

46 → 2 M

CAST ON 8 STITCHES AND KNIT
1 ROUND PLAIN.
ALL ROUNDS WHICH ARE NOT
MENTIONED ARE KNITTED PLAIN.

Design "Monica"

Knitted with DMC Cébélia No. 20
Yarn requirement is about 8 gramme
The stretched size is about 17 centimetre
1 Set of double pointed knitting needles 1.5 millimetre
1 Crochet hook 1.25 millimetre

Crochet edge: Crochet 3-5 stitches together with 7 chain
stitches between.

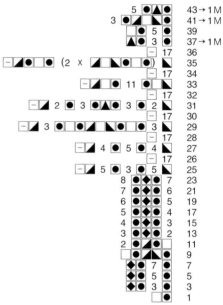

5 ●▲●	43→1M	
3 ●◣◥●	41→1M	
● 5 ●	39	
▲● 3 ●	37→1M	
–	17	36
– ◢● ● (2 x ◢ ◣● ●) ◣	35	
–	17	34
– ◢● ● 11 ● ◣	33	
–	17	32
– ◢ 2 ● 3 ●▲● 3 ● 2 ◣	31	
–	17	30
– ◢ 3 ● ● ◢◣ ●◣ ● ● 3 ◣	29	
–	17	28
– ◢ 4 ● 5 ● 4 ◣	27	
–	17	26
– ◢ 5 ● 3 ● 5 ◣	25	
8 ● ◆ ● 7	23	
7 ● ◆ ● 6	21	
6 ● ◆ ● 5	19	
5 ● ◆ ● 4	17	
4 ● ◆ ● 3	15	
3 ● ◆ ● 2	13	
2 ● ◢▲◣ ●	11	
□ ● ◢◣	9	
◆ ● 7 ●	7	
◆ ● 5 ●	5	
◆ ● 3 ●	3	
□ ●	1	

CAST ON 8 STITCHES AND KNIT
1 ROUND PLAIN.
ALL ROUNDS WHICH ARE NOT
MENTIONED ARE KNITTED PLAIN.

Design "Nadia"

Knitted with DMC Cébélia No. 20
Yarn requirement is about 5 gramme
The stretched size is about 13 centimetre
1 Set of fine knitting needles 1.5 millimetre
1 Crochet hook 1.25 millimetre

Crochet edge: Crochet 3 stitches together
with 7 chain stitches between 5 times, 3 stitches + 1 chain stitch once.

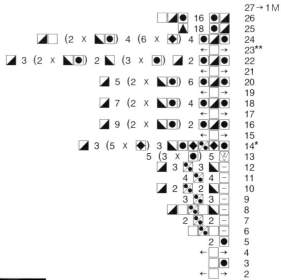

Cast on 8 stitches and knit 1 round plain.
All rounds which are not mentioned are
knitted plain.

NB This design can also be knitted
with 1 plain round between each
pattern line.

* = In round 14 knit 5 stitches tur-
ned plain in the 3 yarn over.

** = In round 23 knit 6 stitches in
the 3 yarn over.

68

Design "Nina"

Knitted with DMC Cébélia No. 30
Yarn requirement is about 10 gramme
The stretched size is about 24 centimetre
1 Set of fine knitting needles 1.5 millimetre
1 Circular needle 1.5 at 40 centimetre
1 Crochet hook 1.25 millimetre

Crochet edge: 1 double crochet + 7 chain stitches in one stitch, 1 double crochet in the next 9 stitches.

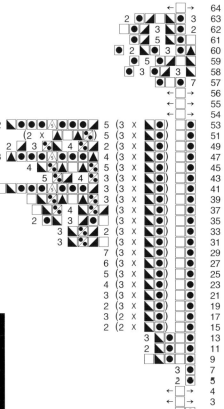

Cast on 8 stitches and knit 1 round plain.
All rounds which are not mentioned are knitted plain.

NB Knit pattern in every round from 57 until round 63.

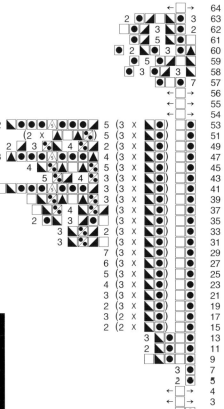

Design "Rikke"

Knitted with DMC Cébélia No. 20
Yarn requirement is about 20 gramme
The stretched size is about 35 centimetre
1 Set of double pointed knitting needles 1.5 millimetre
1 Circular needle 1.5 millimetre at 40 and 50 centimetre
1 Crochet hook 1.25 millimetre

Crochet edge: Crochet 4 stitches together with 7 chain stitches between.

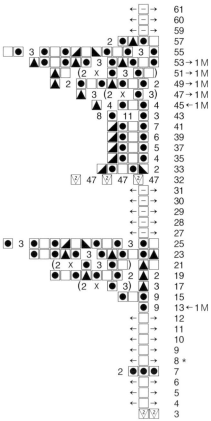

CAST ON 8 STITCHES AND KNIT 2 ROUNDS PLAIN.
ALL ROUNDS WHICH ARE NOT MENTIONED ARE
KNITTED PLAIN.

*** = In round 8 knit 7 stitches in the
3 yarn over.**

70

Design "Rita"

Knitted with DMC Cébélia No. 20
Yarn requirement is about 8 gramme
The stretched size is about 19 centimetre
1 Set of double pointed knitting needles 1.5 millimetre
1 Crochet hook 1.5 millimetre

Crochet edge: Crochet 3 stitches together with 7 chain stitches
between.

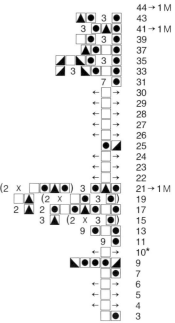

							44→1M
			▲	●	3	●	43
			3	●	▲	●	41→1M
			□		3	●	39
			▲	●		●	37
	▲			●	3	●	35
▲		3	◣	●		●	33
					7	●	31
		←	□	→			30
		←	□	→			29
		←	□	→			28
		←	□	→			27
		←	□	→			26
			●	◢			25
		←	□	→			24
		←	□	→			23
		←	□	→			22
(2 X	□ ● ▲ ●)	3	● ▲	●			21→1M
	▲	(2 X	●	3	●)		19
2	▲	2	●	● ▲	●	●	17
	3	▲	(2 X	3	●)		15
			9	●		●	13
				9		●	11
		←	□	→			10*
	◥	●	●	●	◢		9
						●	7
		←	□	→			6
		←	□	→			5
		←	□	→			4
			□			●	3

CAST ON 8 STITCHES AND KNIT 2
ROUNDS PLAIN.
ALL ROUNDS WHICH ARE NOT MEN-
TIONED ARE KNITTED PLAIN.

*** = In round 10 knit 7 stit-
ches in the 3 yarn over.**

Rosa

Design "Rosa"

Knitted with DMC Cébélia No. 20
Yarn requirement is about 100 gramme
The stretched size is about 80 centimetre
1 Set of double pointed knitting needles 1.5 millimetre
1 Circular needle 1.5 millimetre at 40, 60, 80 and 100 centimetre
1 Crochet hook 1.25 millimetre

to be continued...

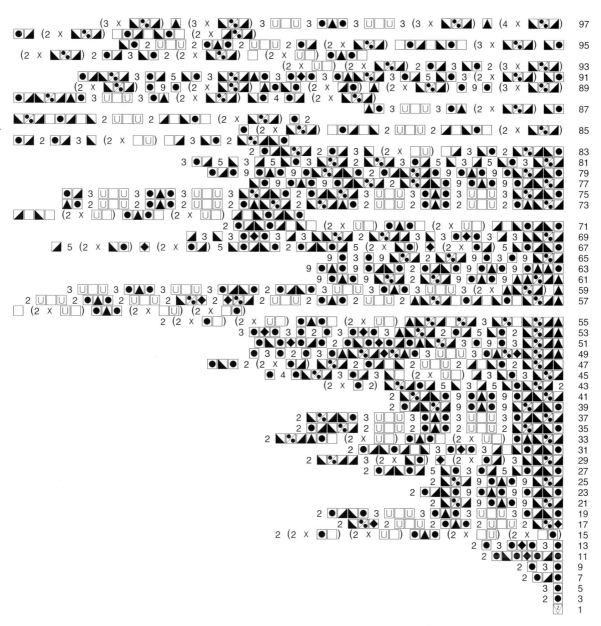

CAST ON 6 STITCHES AND KNIT ONE ROUND PLAIN.
ALL ROUNDS WHICH ARE NOT MENTIONED ARE KNITTED PLAIN.

*= round 144. A total of 516 stitches.

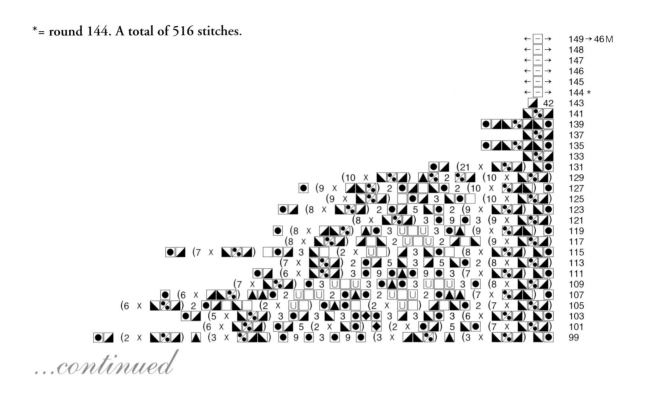

...continued

EDGE - STRAIGHT PART. Repeated 4 times.

Crochet edge: Crochet 5-7-5-7 stitches together with 11 chain stitches between,
5 stitches with 5 chain stitches between, 3 stitches with 5 chain stitches between.

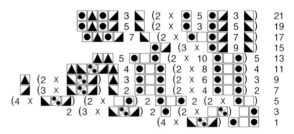

STRAIGHT PIECE. REPEATED 4 TIMES

EDGE - CORNER

Crochet edge: Crochet 5-7-5-7-5-7-5-7 stitches together with 11 chain stitches between,
5 stitches with 5 chain stitches between, 3 stitches with 5 chain stitches between.

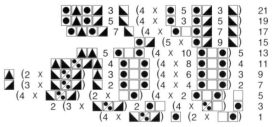

COMMENCE THE FIRST CORNER. PATTERN FOR CORNER.

Design "Sonja"

Knitted with DMC Cébélia No. 20
Yarn requirement is about 20 gramme
The stretched size is about 36 centimetre
1 Set of double pointed knitting needles 1.5 millimetre
1 Circular needle 1.5 millimetre at 40, 50 and 60 centimetre
1 Crochet hook 1.25 millimetre

Crochet edge: Crochet 4 stitches together with 7 chain stitches between.

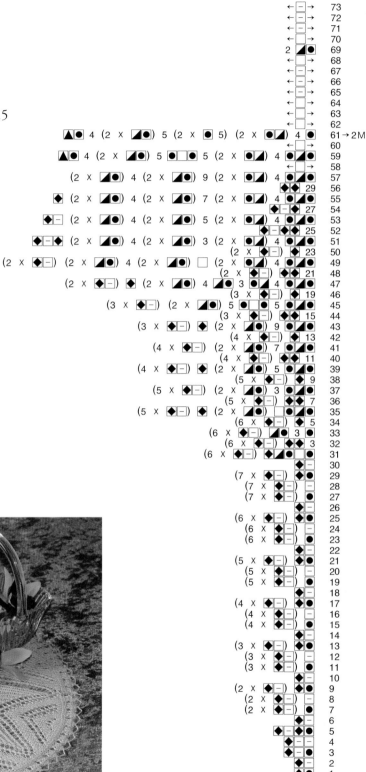

Cast on 8 stitches and knit one plain round.
All rounds which are not mentioned are knitted plain.

75

Design "Tanja"

Knitted with DMC Cébélia No. 20
Yarn requirement is about 10 gramme
The stretched size is about 22 centimetre
1 Set of double pointed knitting needles 1.5 millimetre
1 Crochet hook 1.25 millimetre

Crochet edge: Crochet 2-2-3-3-3-2-2-3 stitches together with
6 chain stitches between.

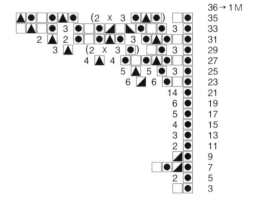

CAST ON 7 STITCHES AND KNIT
2 ROUNDS PLAIN.
ALL ROUNDS WHICH ARE NOT
MENTIONED ARE KNITTED PLAIN.

76

Design "Tove"

Knitted with DMC Cébélia No. 20
Yarn requirement is about 45 gramme
The stretched size is about 44 x 68 centimetre
1 Set of double pointed knitting needles 1.5 millimetre
1 Circular needle 1.5 millimetre at 40 and 50 centimetre
1 Crochet hook 1.25 millimetre

to be continued....

PATTERN **A**

Round 80: The work is split up. Knit 85 stitches and then cast off 170 stitches loosely. Knit 85 stitches and cast off the last 170 stitches loosely. Knit according to pattern B.

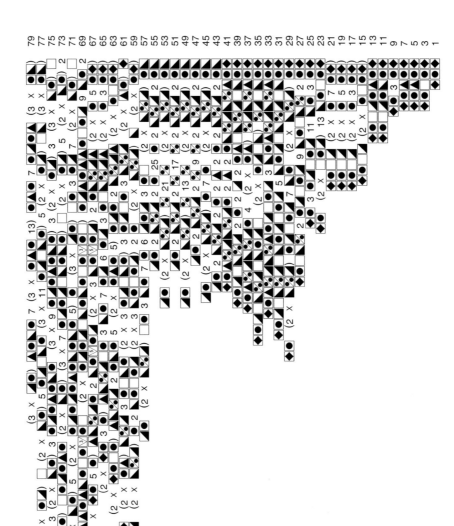

CAST ON 12 STITCHES AND KNIT ONE PLAIN ROUND
ALL ROUNDS WHICH ARE NOT MENTIONED ARE KNITTED PLAIN.

PATTERN B

All stitches are cast off loosely, maybe with a needle 0.5 millimetre larger than the one the design is knitted with, in order not to make the edge too tight.

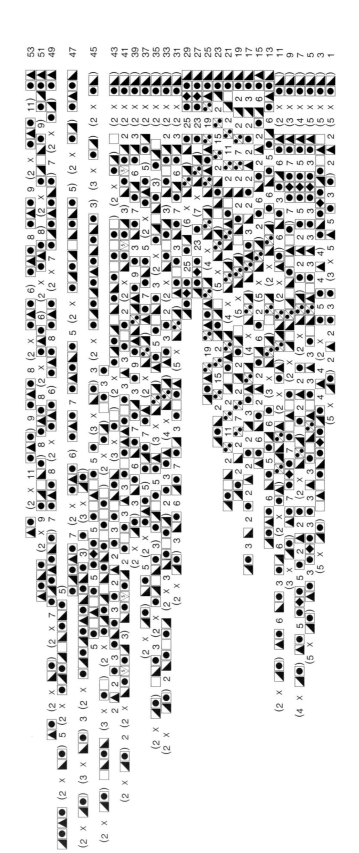

Design "Tut"

Knitted with DMC Cébélia No. 20
Yarn requirement is about 10 gramme
The stretched size is about 25 centimetre
1 Set of double pointed knitting needles 1.5 millimetre
1 Crochet hook 1.5 millimetre

Crochet edge: Crochet 2 stitches together with 5 chain stitches between.

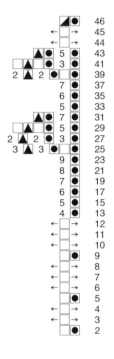

				▲	●		46
			←	□	→		45
			←	□	→		44
		▲	●	5	●		43
	□	▲	●	3	●		41
2	▲	2	●		●		39
			7		●		37
			6		●		35
			5		●		33
	□	▲	●	7	●		31
		▲	●	5	●		29
2	▲	2	●	3	●		27
3	▲	3	●	□			25
			9		●		23
			8		●		21
			7		●		19
			6		●		17
			5		●		15
			4		●		13
	←	□	→				12
	←	□	→				11
	←	□	→				10
		□		●			9
	←	□	→				8
	←	□	→				7
	←	□	→				6
		□		●			5
	←	□	→				4
	←	□	→				3
		□		●			2

CAST ON 6 STITCHES AND KNIT
ONE PLAIN ROUND.
ALL ROUNDS WHICH ARE NOT
MENTIONED ARE KNITTED PLAIN.

Design "Valborg"

Knitted with DMC Cébélia No. 30
Yarn requirement is about 60 gramme
The stretched size is about 58 centimetre
1 Set of double pointed knitting needles 1.5 millimetre
1 Circular needle 1.5 millimetre at 40, 50, 60 and 80 centimetre
1 Crochet hook 1.25 millimetre

to be continued...

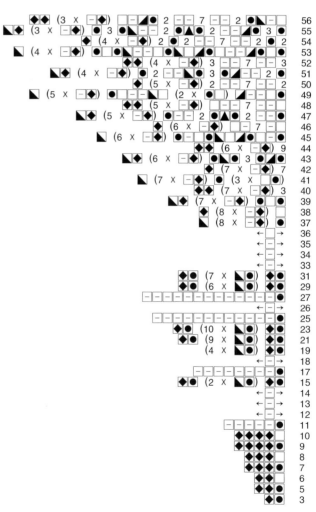

CAST ON 8 STITCHES AND KNIT 2 ROUNDS PLAIN.
ALL ROUNDS WHICH ARE NOT MENTIONED ARE KNITTED PLAIN.

Valborg

to be continued...

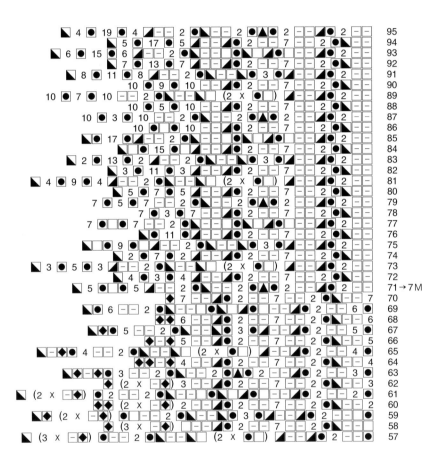

...continued

Crochet edge: Crochet 3 stitches together with 5 chain stitches between.

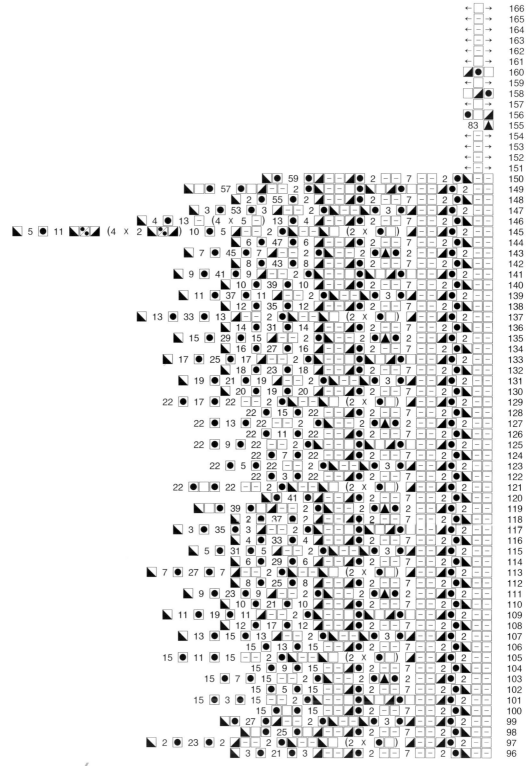

...continued

Design "Vicki"

Knitted with DMC Cébélia No. 20

Yarn requirement is about 6 gramme
The stretched size is about 16 centimetre
1 Set of double pointed knitting needles 1.5 millimetre
1 Crochet hook 1.25 millimetre

Crochet edge: Crochet 3 stitches together with 6 chain stitches between.
Round 2: 7 chain stitches between each chain.

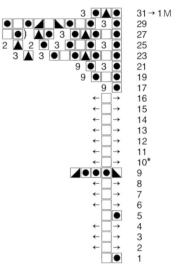

CAST ON 8 STITCHES AND KNIT
ONE ROUND PLAIN.
ALL ROUNDS WHICH ARE NOT
MENTIONED ARE KNITTED PLAIN.

*** = In round 10 knit 7 stitches
in the 3 yarn over.**

Design "Åse"

Knitted with DMC Cébélia No. 20
Yarn requirement is about 10 gramme
The stretched size is about 23 centimetre
1 Set of double pointed knitting needles 1.5 millimetre
1 Crochet hook 1.25 millimetre

Crochet edge: Crochet 2-2-3-3-3-3-3-2-2-3 stitches together with 7 chain stitches between.

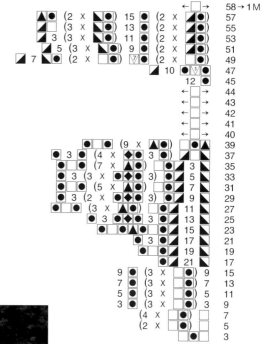

CAST ON 6 STITCHES AND KNIT
2 ROUNDS PLAIN.
ALL ROUNDS WHICH ARE NOT
MENTIONED ARE KNITTED PLAIN.